THE WHIMSICAL WATERCOLOR ART OF LAUREL NELSON

FOR
HELEN CUMMINS

THANK YOU

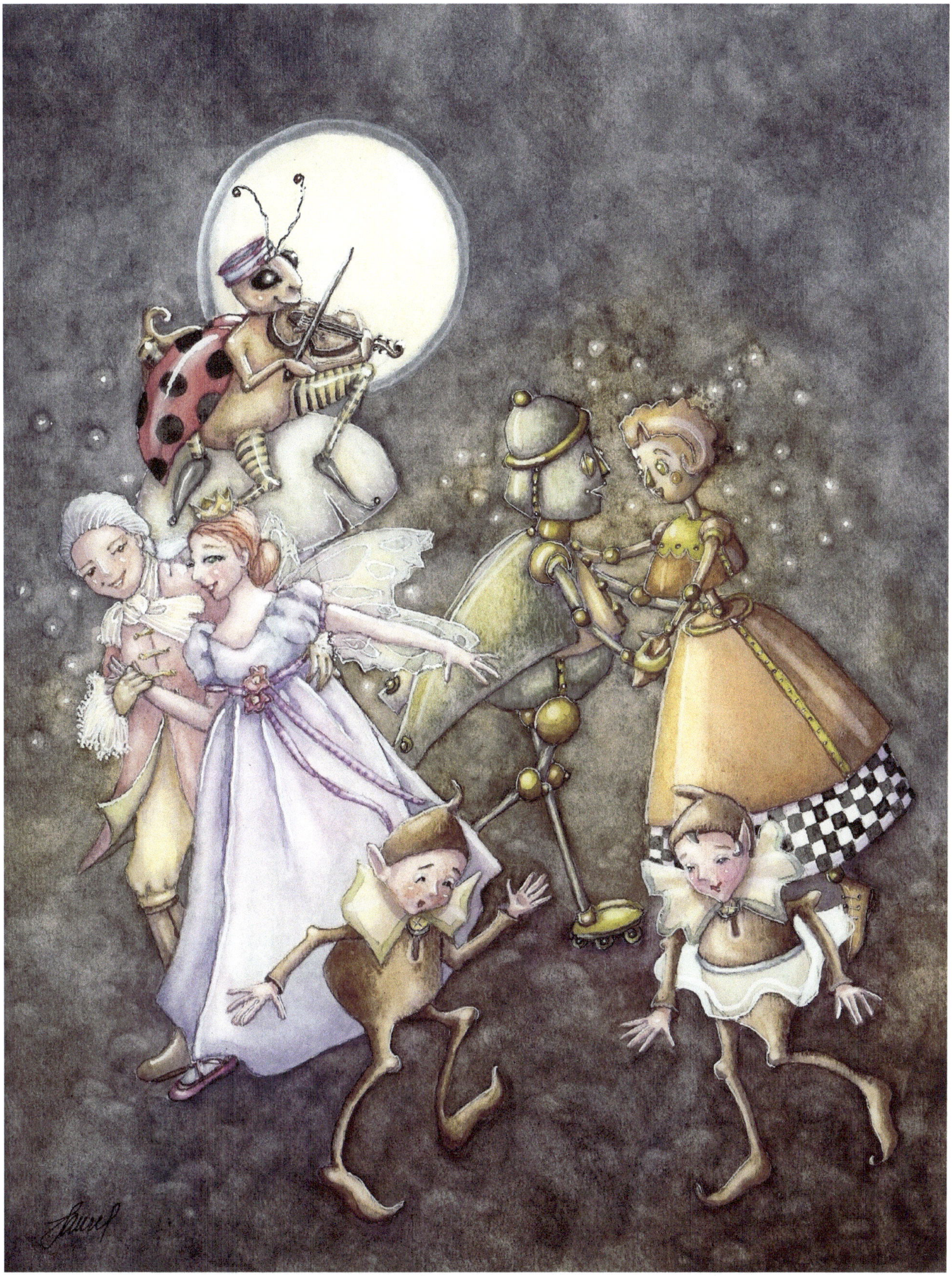

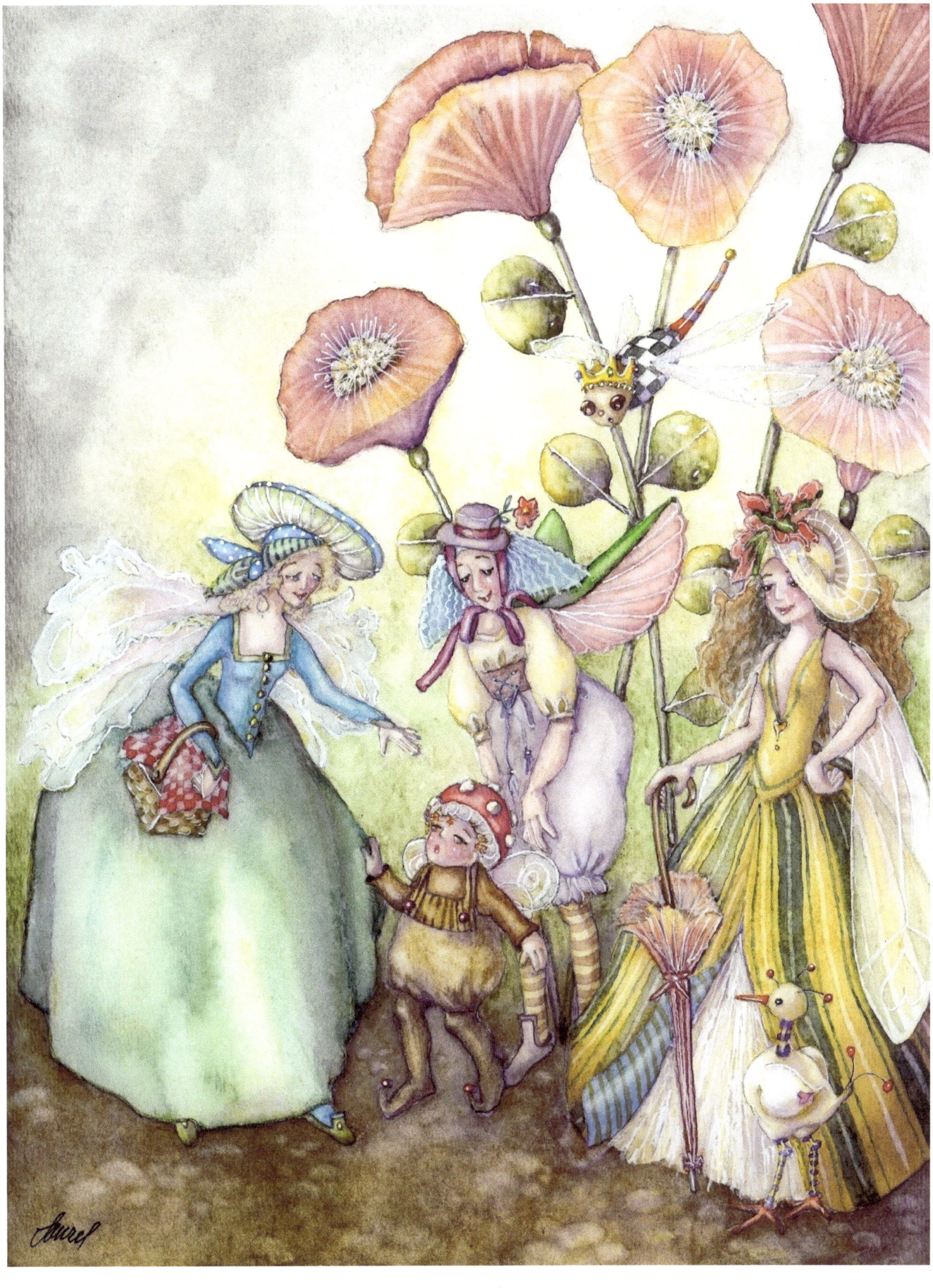
Laurel

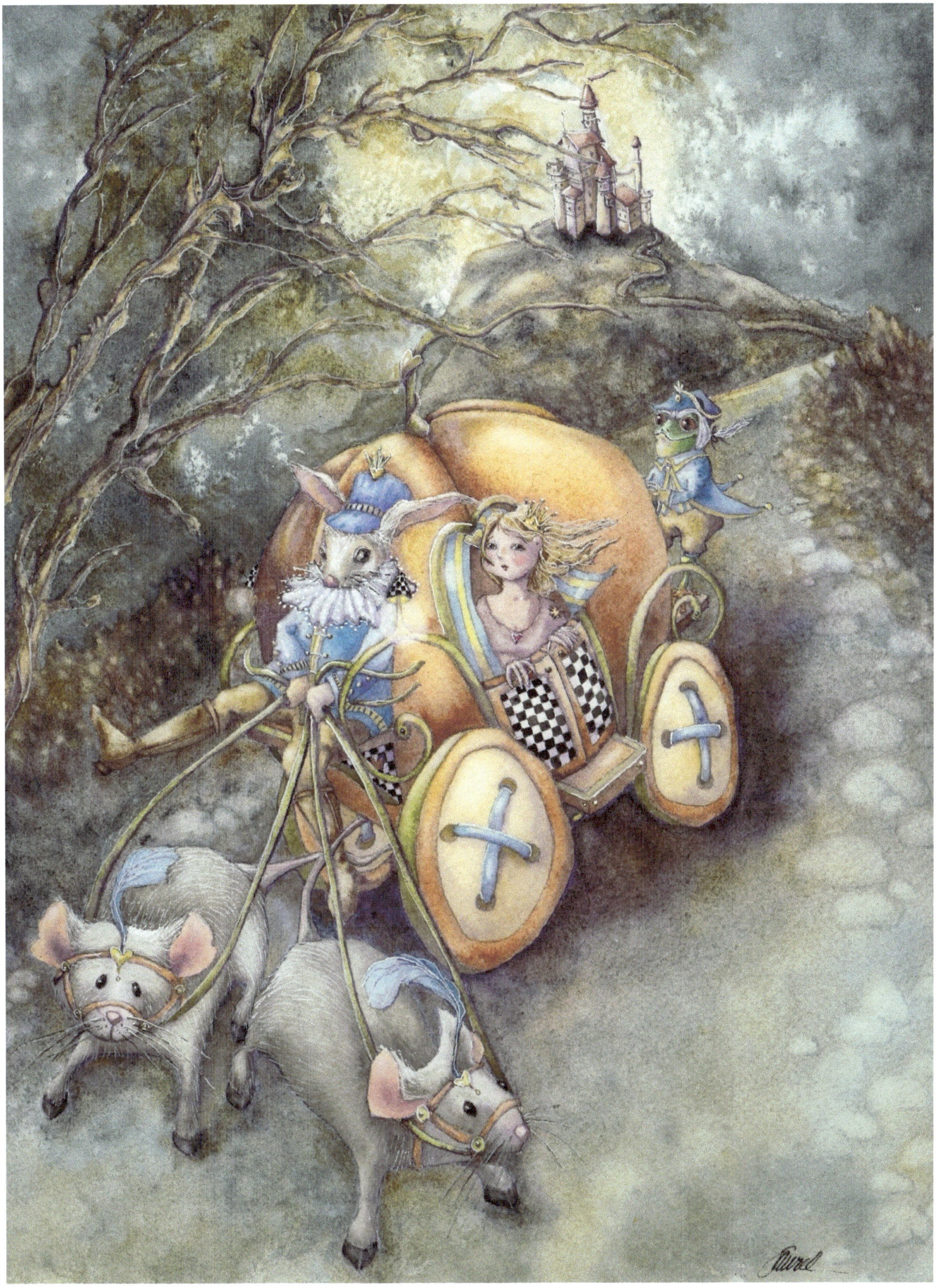

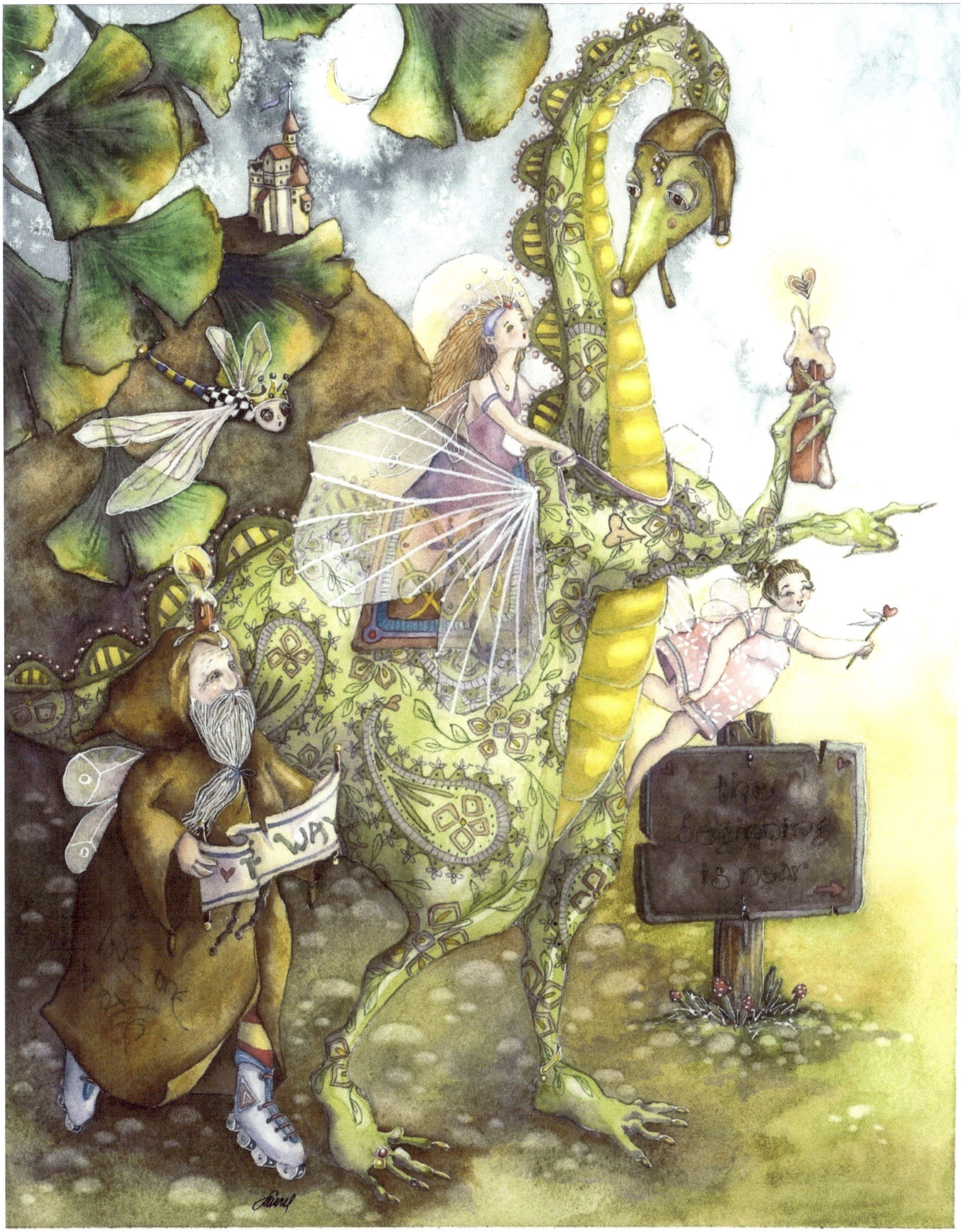
the beginning is near
WAY

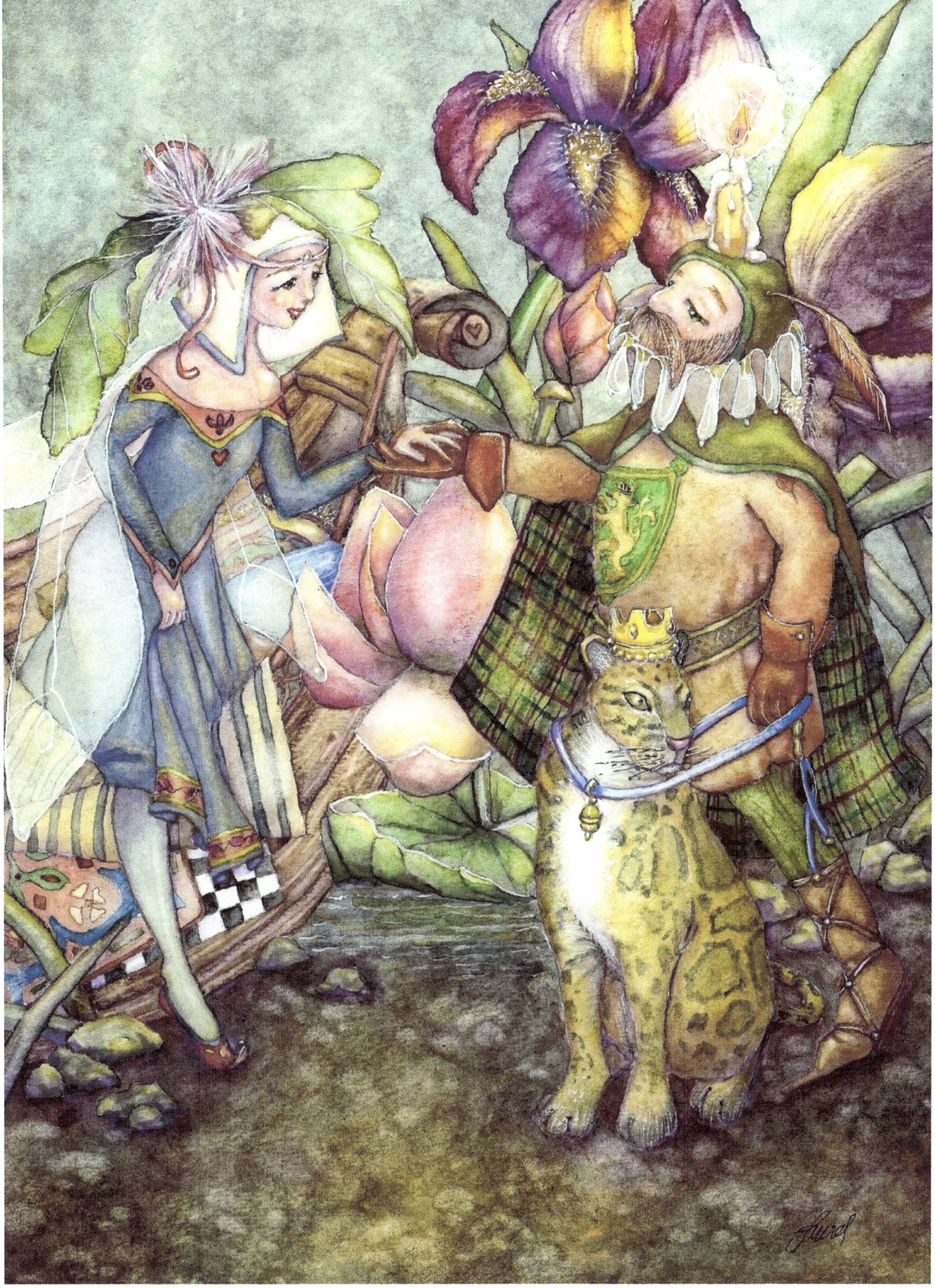

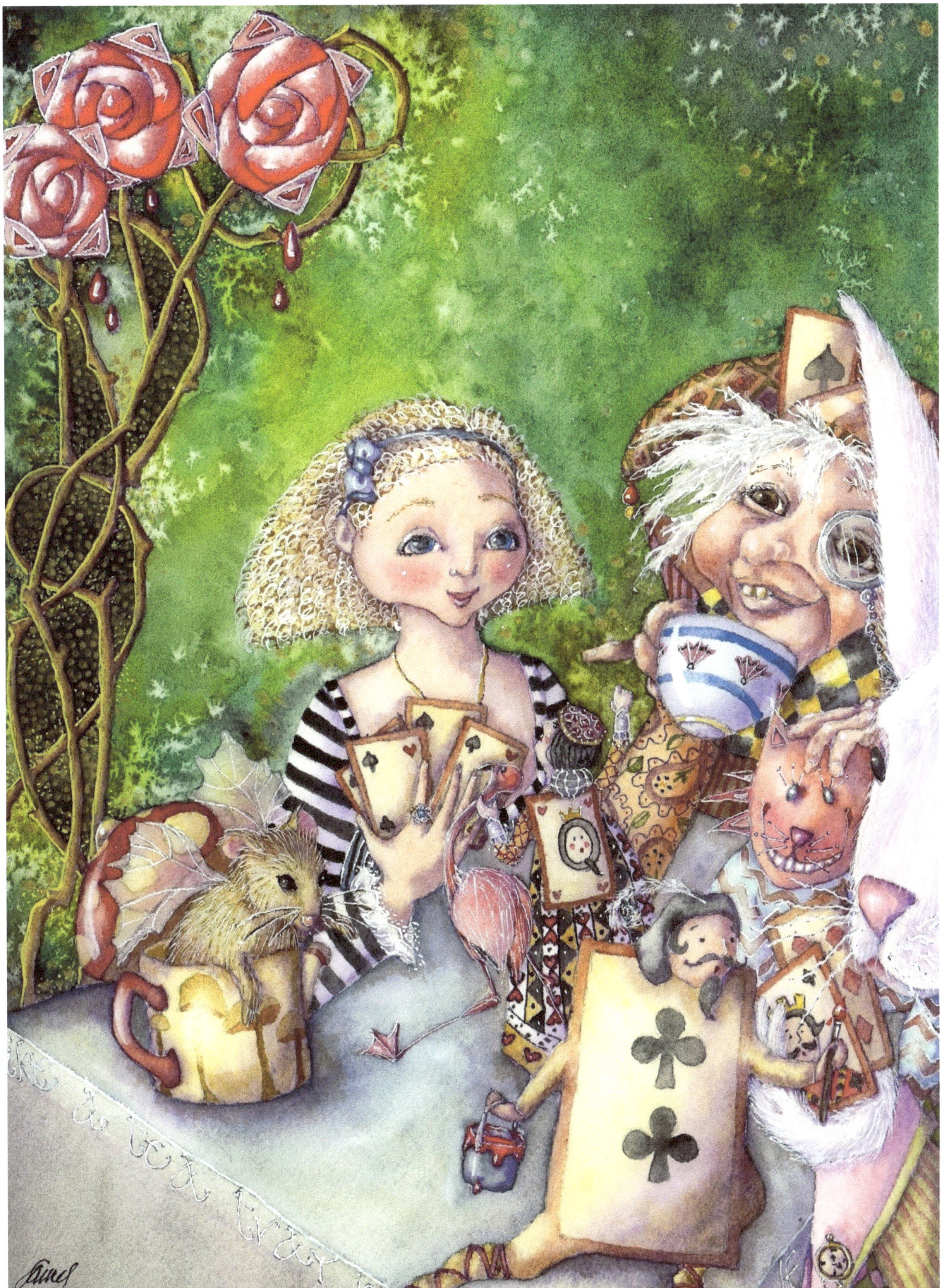

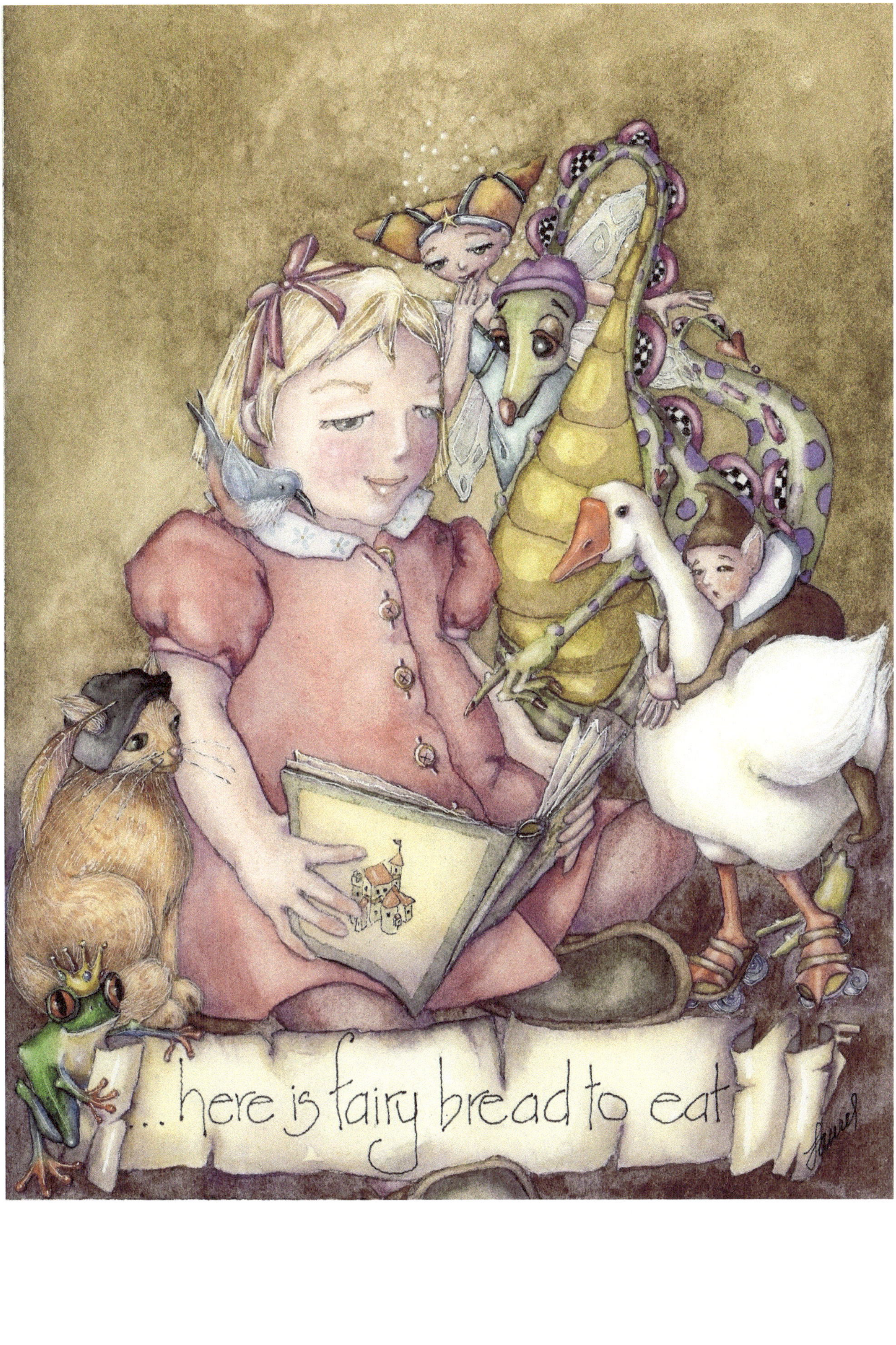
. . . here is fairy bread to eat

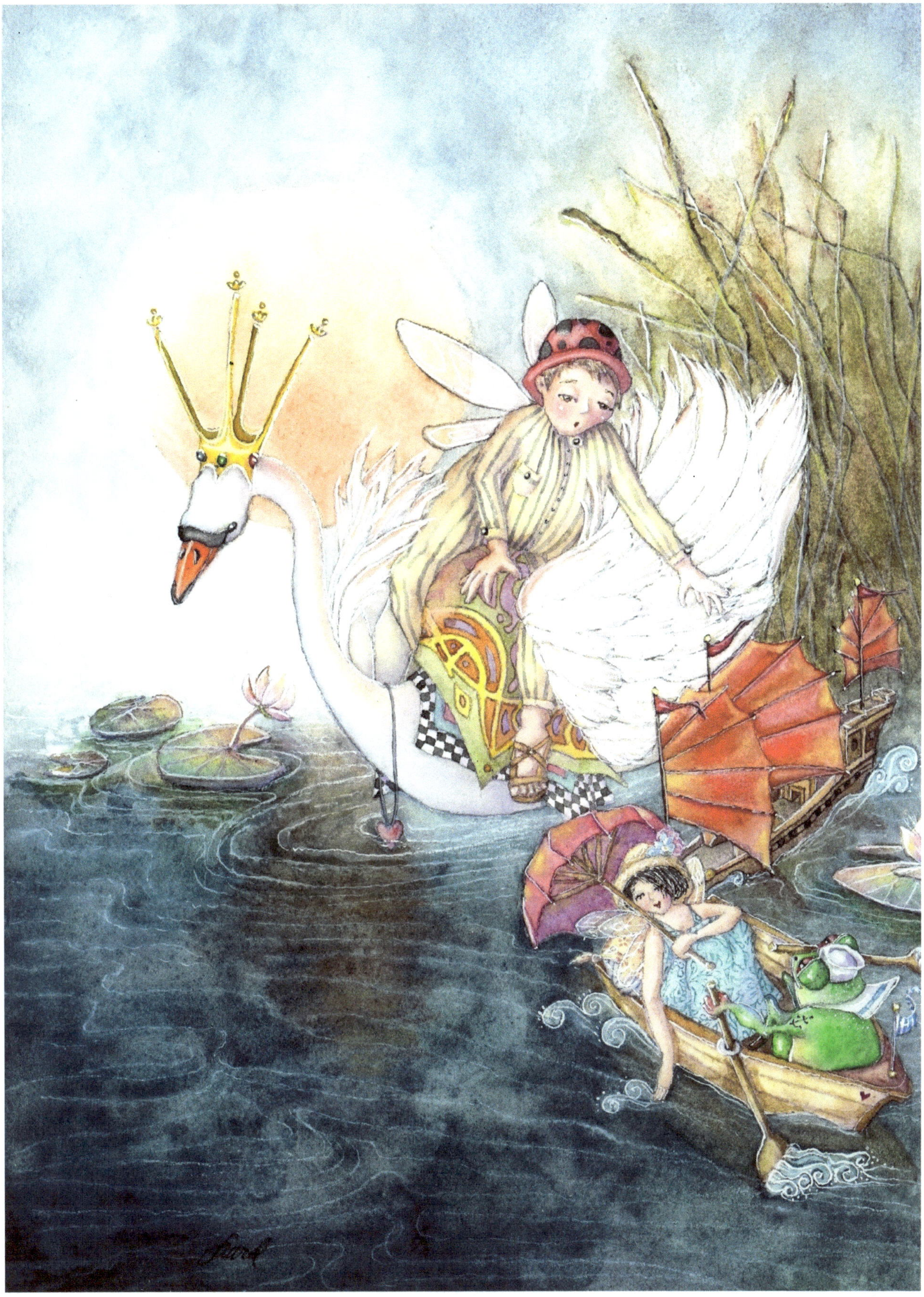

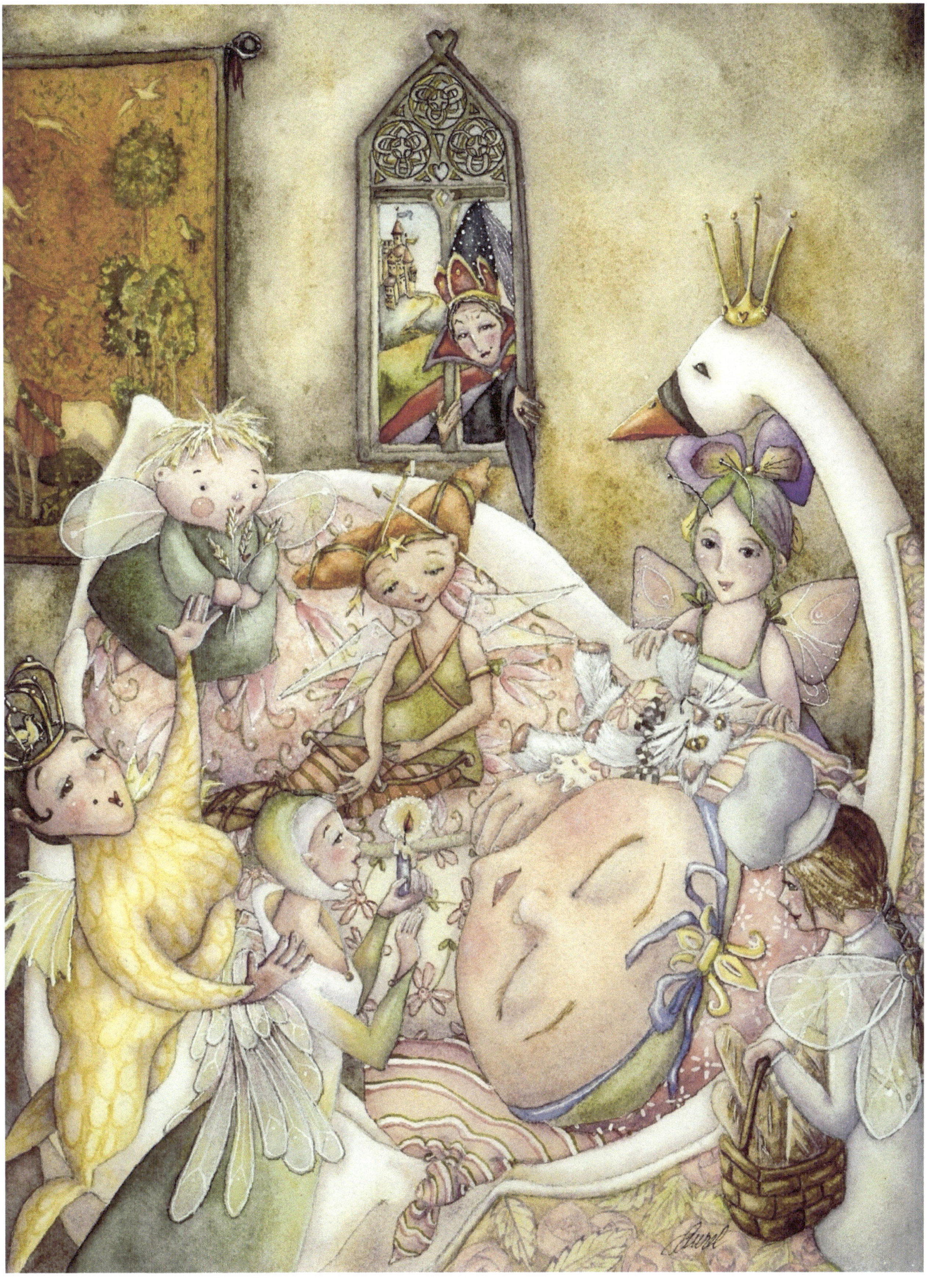

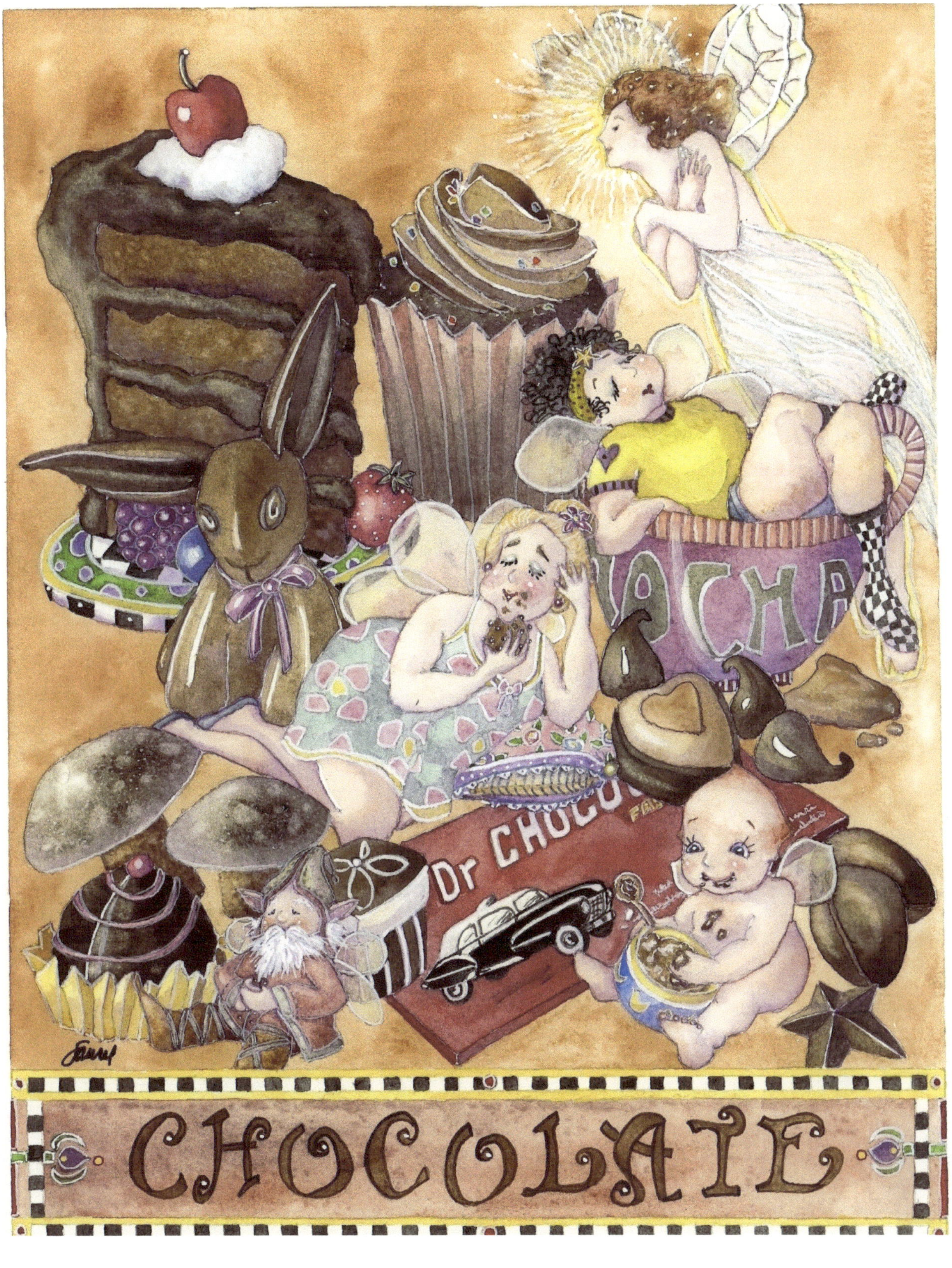
CHOCOLATE

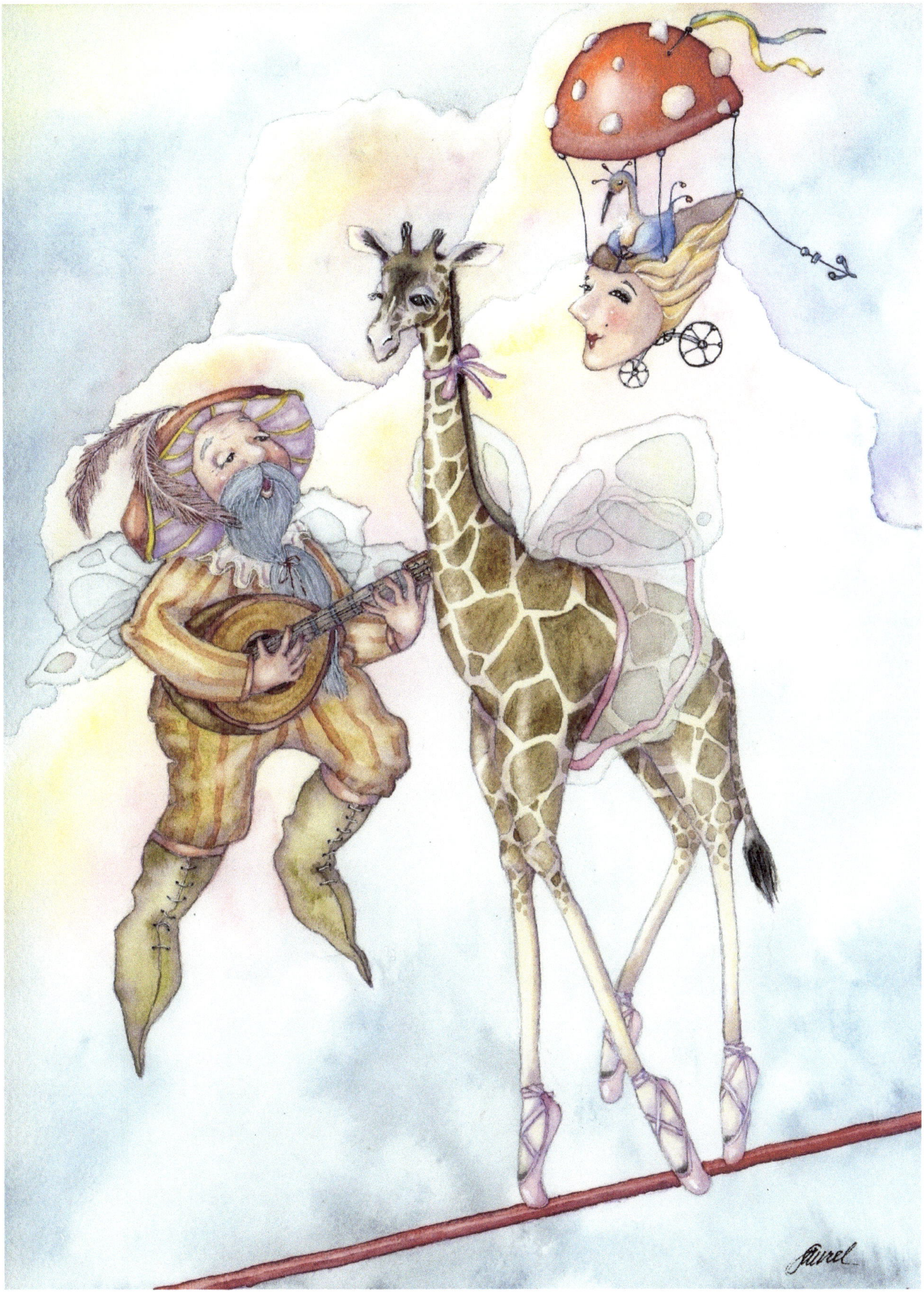

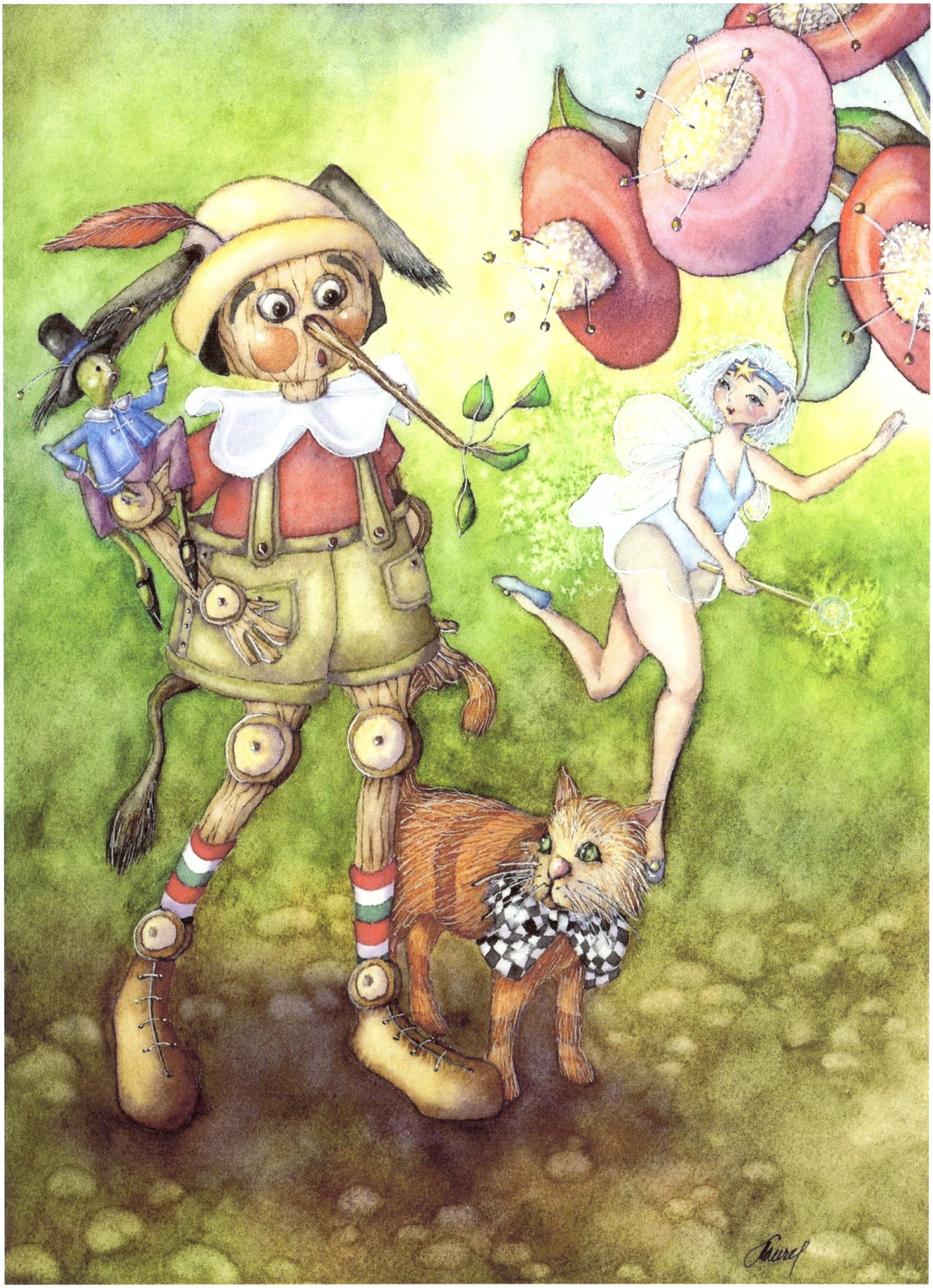

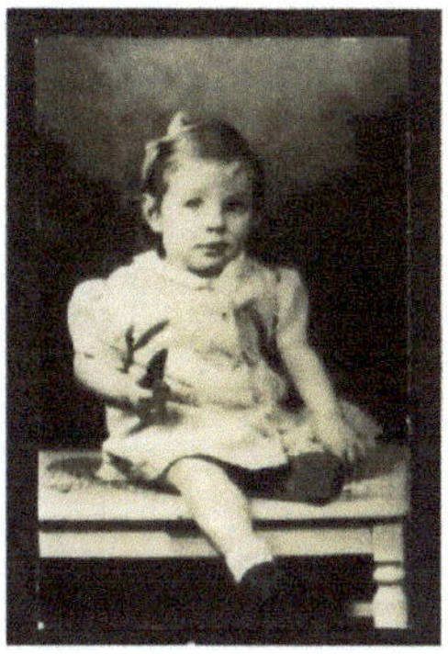

LAURELADEL@GMAIL.COM

laurelnelsonwhimsy.imagekind.com

www.ingramcontent.com/pod-product-compliance
Lightning Source LLC
Chambersburg PA
CBHW050422180526
45159CB00005B/2380
* 9 7 8 1 5 3 7 3 9 4 0 3 9 *